essential careers™

CAREERS AS A
FIRST
RESPONDER

GINA HAGLER

ROSEN
PUBLISHING®

NEW YORK

To Jason, Seth, and Tess—the greatest team in the world!

Published in 2013 by The Rosen Publishing Group, Inc.
29 East 21st Street, New York, NY 10010

First Edition

Library of Congress Cataloging-in-Publication Data

Hagler, Gina.
Careers as a first responder/Gina Hagler.—1st ed.
    p. cm.—(Essential careers)
Includes bibliographical references and index.
ISBN 978-1-4488-8234-2 (library binding)
1. Emergency medical technicians—Juvenile literature. 2. Emergency medical services—Juvenile literature. 3. First responders—Juvenile literature. I. Title.
RA645.5.H34 2013
362.18—dc23

                                                                2012010253

Manufactured in the United States of America

CPSIA Compliance Information: Batch #W13YA: For further information, contact Rosen Publishing, New York, New York, at 1-800-237-9932.

contents

INTRO

In a disaster, first responders can come from around the world to lend assistance. Here, a French team brings an injured American out of the ruins of a collapsed hotel in Haiti.

DUCTION

I t's difficult to see what an earthquake in Haiti, a mine collapse in Bolivia, a levee break in New Orleans, and a youth camp shooting in Norway could have in common. After all, these are different types of events. They occurred around the world. Yet all of them do have something in common. The people who rushed to the sites of these emergencies were first responders.

First responders are at work around the globe. They are the disaster relief workers, rescue teams, and medical personnel who are the first to sort through the chaos in a life-threatening emergency. They are the ones who look for survivors and provide the immediate care they require.

In good economic times and bad, first responders are a vital part of any community. Their jobs are largely recession-proof. Emergencies and disasters don't stop occurring when economic conditions are bad. There is always a need for those who will help others in immediate need of assistance. Some organizations that employ first responders are not completely safe from budget cuts. In bad economic times, many ambulance services and rescue squads may need to cut back on the number of first responders they employ. They may do this by encouraging early retirement, putting a freeze on hiring, or cutting some positions. Whatever the case, talented, hard-working people will still be needed.

You've no doubt seen first responders racing to a call. They may be the EMTs aboard an ambulance, Red Cross workers creating a place where displaced persons can safely stay, or

Sam Gray is a member of Virginia Task Force 1. This elite team specializes in global emergency response. The team assisted the injured after the earthquake in Haiti in 2010.

search-and-rescue teams at work in helicopters or on the ground with specially trained dogs. They are all an integral part of the emergency medical services (EMS) system at the international, federal, state, or local level. They respond to emergency situations such as floods, earthquakes, tsunamis, terrorist attacks, and train crashes.

Some first responders have national certification. This means they have completed the curriculum set out by the federal government to earn certification and passed a national certification exam. All first responders have licensure at the state level to respond to emergencies in their area.

When considering career options, individuals should think about the type of job they want. A career as a first responder is challenging because the work hours vary, and the conditions from call to call are rarely the same. It is rewarding because a first responder helps people in dire need. For anyone who is willing to take risks and wants a steady, fast-paced job with good benefits, working alongside others who are dedicated to helping those in trouble, a career as a first responder might be just right.

chapter 1

HAVING A CAREER AS A FIRST RESPONDER

First responders are the people who rush to the site of an emergency or disaster. They stabilize the injured for the trip to a medical facility. They are also the professionals who search for people in wilderness areas and in collapsed structures. Both types of first responders supply prehospital care to the injured.

EMTs AND PARAMEDICS

Emergency medical technicians (EMTs) and paramedics are two types of first responders. These emergency medical services (EMS) professionals rush to situations ranging from automobile accidents and heart attacks to births and gunshot incidents. They care for the person in need of assistance and transport that person to a medical facility.

EMTs and paramedics are on call through 9-1-1 systems around the country. When they arrive on-site, they assess the

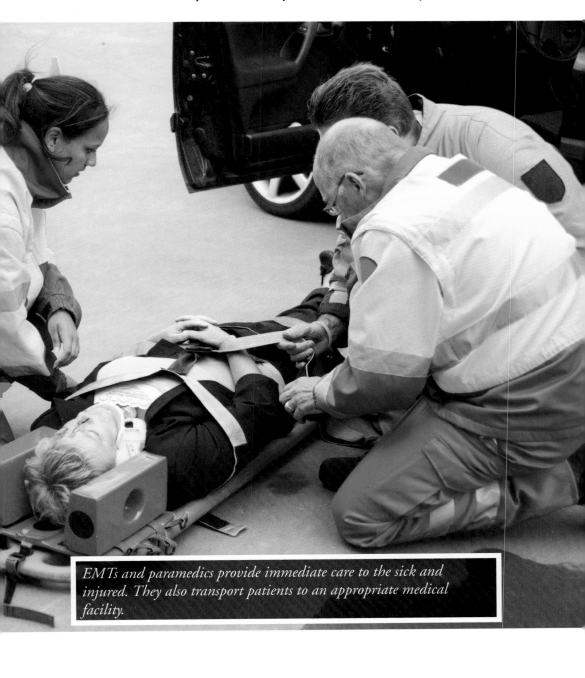

EMTs and paramedics provide immediate care to the sick and injured. They also transport patients to an appropriate medical facility.

patient's condition, learn any background medical information they can under the circumstances, stabilize the patient, and transport the patient to a medical facility. They provide emergency medical care at the site as well as along the way. It is their role to meet the patient's immediate needs. In some systems, the EMTs and paramedics are in touch with doctors at the medical facility while they are en route. When this is the case, they will follow the directions of the doctor.

Once they arrive at the medical facility, first responders bring their patients into the emergency room (ER). They brief the medical personnel there and document the case before restocking the ambulance and preparing for their next call. This includes decontaminating the ambulance if the patient had a communicable disease and alerting the proper authorities when it is required.

EMTs and paramedics work in a rolling medical facility— the ambulance. On board they have equipment to monitor a patient's vital signs and take care of a range of injuries and conditions, including preliminary care of wounds and breathing difficulties. They also have backboards so that they can immobilize those patients who have suffered serious trauma to the back and neck. EMTs and paramedics work as part of a team. Often one team member will drive while the other monitors vital signs and sits in the back of the ambulance with the injured person.

Earning certification as an emergency medical technician (EMT) requires many hours of training and experience. There is also ongoing education for this essential and challenging career.

Many EMTs and paramedics work with ambulances, but others are members of helicopter crews. Duties similar to those in ambulances are performed before a patient is airlifted to the appropriate medical facility. Some EMS personnel work for private ambulance services or private companies, too.

EMTs and paramedics perform additional duties according to their level of certification. As an organized profession, EMS is still developing, and the National Highway Traffic Safety Administration (NHTSA) is transitioning to a system with four practice levels: emergency medical responder (EMR), emergency medical technician (EMT), advanced emergency medical technician (AEMT), and paramedic.

According to federal government definitions, emergency medical responders possess the basic knowledge and skills to begin lifesaving care while awaiting additional EMS response. They perform basic interventions with minimal equipment. People certified as emergency medical technicians (formerly known as EMT-basic) have the skills to manage respiratory, cardiac, and trauma emergencies. They provide basic life support (BLS) with the basic equipment found on an ambulance. Advanced emergency medical technicians (formerly known as EMT-intermediate) require additional training. The care that an advanced emergency medical technician may provide varies state by state.

Paramedics carry out not only the procedures of the other levels but also administer medications orally (by mouth) and intravenously (by way of a vein), read electrocardiograms (EKGs), perform intubations, and use and monitor complex equipment. They are able to perform advanced life support (ALS). Their specific duties also vary by state.

A career as an EMT or paramedic involves a great deal of physical activity. These first responders need to lift patients, kneel beside them as they make their assessments, and do what is necessary to deliver emergency medical care. They may also be exposed to communicable diseases such as hepatitis B and AIDS. Some of the calls involve combative patients or work under stressful conditions with patients who are in pain. There

First responders regularly train for man-made and natural disasters. Here, members of California Task Force 2, an urban search-and-rescue team, unload for a simulated mission involving a 6.7-magnitude earthquake.

is often considerable noise and even the possibility of hearing loss caused by sirens and other emergency signals. The responsibility of caring for people who require immediate emergency medical assistance on shifts that cover twenty-four-hour periods is not for everyone. As a result, there is a high burnout and turnover rate in EMS positions, with people frequently leaving to be replaced by others.

SEARCH AND RESCUE

Search-and-rescue (SAR) personnel work on teams that are deployed to find and provide aid to those who are injured or in danger. The type of search-and-rescue team and the equipment they use varies with the population and the terrain. Urban search-and-rescue teams locate and rescue people from collapsed buildings or other hazardous urban situations. These teams are often referred to as heavy urban search-and-rescue (HUSAR) teams and include police, fire, and emergency medical services personnel. An important part of HUSAR training is learning about dangers such as the live electrical wires and broken natural gas lines that are often associated with structural collapse.

Wilderness search and rescue (WSAR) often includes work in mountainous areas. Because of the rugged terrain and large areas that must be covered quickly, helicopters are often used as part of the search. Helicopters are also used to quickly bring the patient to a medical facility. Search dogs—and their handlers— are frequently members of the team. Many national parks in the United States employ professional search-and-rescue teams.

Swiftwater search-and-rescue teams operate along rivers and other inland waterways. These first responders are trained to reach and rescue those involved in life-threatening mishaps. They are also trained to provide medical assistance on the way to a medical facility. Coast guard search-and-rescue professionals provide aid to those who are injured on the open water or ocean. They respond with small boats called cutters and often use helicopters in their operations as well.

Canine search-and-rescue teams employ specially trained dogs and their handlers. The

Extricating injured rock climbers requires rescuers who not only have the medical skills to treat the injured but also the rock climbing skills to reach the injured.

HEAR WHAT FIRST RESPONDERS HAVE TO SAY

The training is tough, the hours are difficult, and the work is dangerous. Why would anyone choose to be a first responder?

- "I don't like to sit still for too long," said Tim Moyer, graduate of the EMT program at Skyline College in San Bruno, California, in a video interview for GoIntoHealthcare.org. "[I like] getting out and doing things—lifting, moving, talking, and having to think on the fly. You've got this patient who's showing these symptoms. What's wrong? What can we do to stabilize them to transport them? Do we need additional help? Don't we? Being able to think for yourself and do things for yourself is great."

- "Our active members love being in the outdoors, regardless of conditions," said Harrison Ripps of the Central Massachusetts Search and Rescue Team in an interview with Philip Werner of SectionHiker.com. "We take team safety seriously, but people generally don't go missing when the weather's warm and the skies are clear, so you have to be OK with rain and cold. Also, people who stick with the team long-term are less interested in glory and more interested in being thorough. Our active members are easy-going team players—when you are on a search and time is of the essence, you have to be able to check your ego at the door."

- "We get to the call and such a wide variety of things can happen," said EMS-paramedic Brayden Hamilton-Smith in an interview for Toronto EMS Info Cast, a YouTube channel devoted to emergency medical services in Toronto, Canada. "It might be a traumatic call. It might involve administering medications or managing a fracture, some bleeding, a burn, or anything like that. Each call is different."

dogs locate people who are trapped in the rubble of buildings or in other remote locations. When a person is found, the rescue operation is taken over by those trained to extricate people and provide medical care until a medical facility can be reached.

The one thing these different types of search-and-rescue teams have in common is their dedication to rapid response and decisive action in the event of an emergency. The training involved for team members varies to match the environment,

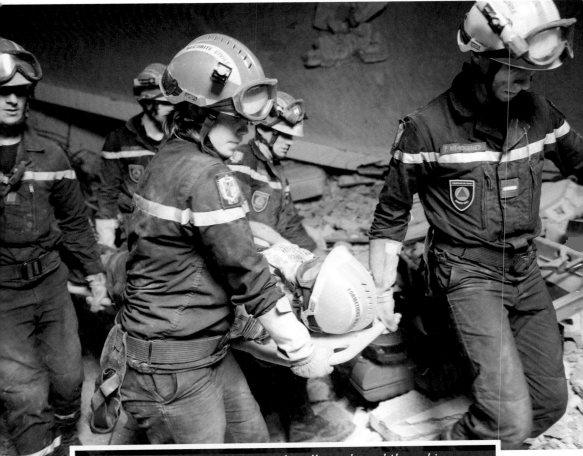

Search-and-rescue teams must work well together while making personal safety and the safety of the injured their top priorities.

but all of them must be able to reach the injured party and provide a basic to advanced level of medical care before a patient reaches a medical facility. The level of care provided depends on the training of the particular responder.

First responders often work in difficult locations under severe conditions. Members of Virginia Task Force 1 search for survivors in Ofunato, Japan, which was badly damaged in the 2011 earthquake and tsunami.

To carry out search-and-rescue duties, first responders must be in excellent physical condition. The terrain is often difficult. Conditions are often hazardous. First responders must be agile and able to bend, lift, and carry heavy loads. They must be physically fit so that they can hike into the backcountry or make their way across swiftwater or flooding.

The ability to work as part of a team is essential to a search-and-rescue first responder. These teams are multitalented. Individuals with different skills come together for the common goal of locating and extricating the injured party. A first responder in these circumstances must have good communication skills, work well with others, and be flexible enough to adapt to changing circumstances.

Inclement weather often plays a significant role in search-and-rescue operations. First responders must be able to act and think quickly in extreme heat and cold. They also must be able to adapt to conditions following a natural disaster, such as a hurricane or tornado. They may deal with injured individuals who are far from the nearest medical facility. They must be willing and able to take on the responsibility for their care until a medical facility can be reached.

INTERNATIONAL SEARCH AND RESCUE

Not all search-and-rescue teams act only in their own countries. There are teams from around the world that will travel wherever they are needed. In the United States, there are a number of search-and-rescue teams, called task forces, that assist in international disasters.

Virginia Task Force 1 (VA-TF1) is an international urban search-and-rescue team operating out of Fairfax, Virginia. Virginia Task Force 1 has nearly two hundred specially trained rescue personnel. These trained career and volunteer fire and rescue personnel have the expertise required to come to the aid of victims of collapsed structures following natural or man-made catastrophes.

California Task Force 2 (CA-TF2) is an international urban search-and-rescue team operating out of Los Angeles County, California. California Task Force 2 has a seventy-person team that stands ready to respond to international disasters, whether man-made or natural.

These elite task forces are made up of firefighters, paramedics, rescue specialists, emergency room physicians, structural engineers, heavy equipment specialists, K-9 search dogs and their handlers, hazardous materials technicians, communications specialists, and logistics specialists. Members undergo rigorous training. They must have excellent teamwork and communication skills, as well as the ability to carry the equipment they need to the disaster site.

chapter 2

EDUCATION, TRAINING, AND SOURCES OF TRAINING

Any profession that requires its members to make life-and-death decisions while working under pressure requires specialized training. It also requires certification and licensing. The specific type of training, certification, and licensing varies by state. It also varies according to the specific role an individual plays on a team and which skills are needed to do the job. However, all first responders need to master the same basics. They must also take refresher and continuing education courses throughout their careers. Sample or unofficial copies of the certification tests can be found at the Web sites of the National Registry of Emergency Medical Technicians (NREMT) and the National Association for Search & Rescue (NASAR), as well as in study guides sold in bookstores.

TRAINING FOR EMTs AND PARAMEDICS

A high school diploma or GED and a satisfactory background check are first steps to a career as a first responder. The next step is emergency medical training at one of a number of levels.

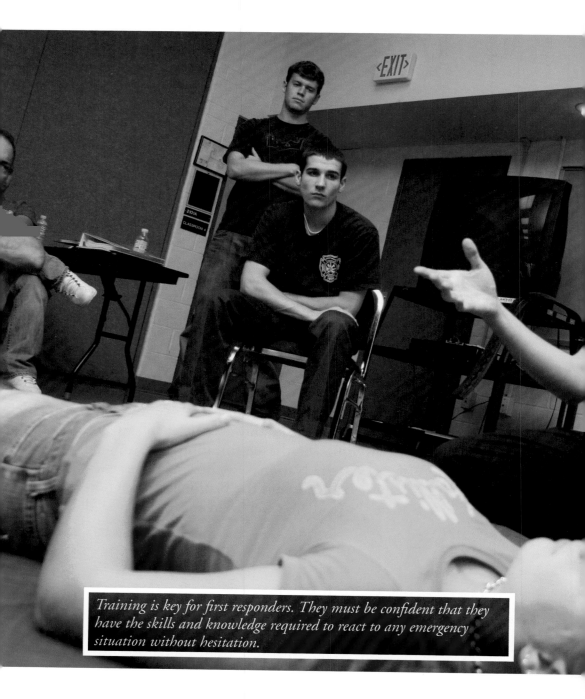

Training is key for first responders. They must be confident that they have the skills and knowledge required to react to any emergency situation without hesitation.

Emergency medical technician training (formerly known as EMT-basic) prepares candidates to assess patients; manage respiratory problems, trauma, and cardiac emergencies; and deal with bleeding, fractures, airway obstruction, and emergency childbirth. Time in an ER or on an ambulance is often part of the course. Students also learn how to use and care for equipment such as backboards and stretchers. These EMTs can deliver basic life support. Upon graduation, there is a written and practical exam given by the National Registry of Emergency Medical Technicians and/or the state licensing agency.

Advanced EMT training (formerly known as EMT-intermediate) varies by state. The nationally defined requirements generally include 30 to 350 hours of training, with the exact amount of training dependent upon the specific responsibilities of the job. Some of the skills that students learn during training include the use of intravenous fluids and certain medications.

EMT CERTIFICATION TEST: SAMPLE QUESTIONS

Each level of certification is awarded after a candidate successfully completes the test for that level. Here's a sampling of the questions for emergency medical technician (EMT-basic) certification from the Web site EMT-National-Training.com (http://www.emt-national-training.com/practice_tests.php):

1. **Medical control has ordered you to assist a patient with a metered dose inhaler. Before assisting this patient, you must ensure what?**
   a. It's not leaking.
   b. It is the patient's medication and is within the expiration date.
   c. The person is not choking.
   d. The hospital has more of the same medication for arrival.

2. **Epinephrine administered for severe allergic reaction may cause?**
   a. Vomiting
   b. Nausea
   c. Chest pain
   d. All of the above

3. **Your patient is a 69-year-old female who has a history of diabetes. She is breathing very deeply and very rapidly in a state of respiratory acidosis. Her husband said he woke up to her breathing like this and she would not wake up. You know that this woman is most likely in?**
   a. Respiratory rebound stage
   b. A diabetic coma
   c. Diabetic shock
   d. Respiratory alkalosis

EMT CERTIFICATION TEST: SAMPLE QUESTIONS (CONT.)

4. **You arrive on-scene to an unknown injury or illness. Your initial impression of the patient leads you to check for arm drift. What are you looking for?**
    a. Proper mentation
    b. Stroke signs
    c. Signs of depression
    d. Arm abrasions

5. **The endocrine system**
    a. Involves the fingernails and skin
    b. Is responsible for hemoglobin transport
    c. Is a rarely used system in the autonomic structure
    d. Produces hormones and secretes them into the blood

6. **A patient who requires restraints should always be**
    a. Transported prone in case he or she vomits
    b. Transported supine
    c. Strapped to a backboard and bagged with a BVM
    d. Held with pressure from the knee to the middle of the back

7. **A patient is complaining of difficulty breathing after being struck in the ribs by a baseball and is cyanotic around the lips. Proper action would include**
    a. Sweeping the tongue out of the way to look for airway obstructions
    b. High-flow 0_2 via NRB and rapid transport
    c. BVM with supplemental oxygen attached
    d. Advice on proper use of a mitt

    Answers: B, D, B, B, D, B, B

Paramedic training is the most advanced level of emergency medical training. In preparing for the rigors and responsibility of this career, the coursework can take up to two years. Often the program is conducted at community colleges or technical schools and may result in an associate's degree. As part of the coursework, students learn about anatomy and physiology. They also acquire advanced medical skills. A significant amount of field and clinical experience is required. Paramedics can deliver advanced life support. Upon graduation, the candidate will take the NREMT examination and become certified as a paramedic.

All fifty states require EMTs and paramedics to be licensed. The levels and titles vary from state to state, but most states and the District of Columbia require certification by the NREMT. Some states have their own certification exams, too. Usually licenses must be renewed every two to three years. EMTs and paramedics are also expected to take refresher courses or meet continuing education requirements.

APPRENTICESHIPS

Some states offer apprenticeships for first responder positions. These apprenticeships satisfy on-the-job training requirements and are part of the training for certification. Some states require the candidate to take a civil service exam and be hired by the fire district before becoming an apprentice, while others do not. Either way, an apprenticeship is a job that requires the candidate to show up on time and do his or her work as directed. Depending on the way the apprenticeship program is structured in the state, some apprentices will receive pay during the last part of their apprenticeship, and some will not. All apprentices have the opportunity to experience the work they plan to do as they develop the skills they'll need.

SEARCH-AND-RESCUE TRAINING

There are a number of training programs and certifications available to search-and-rescue first responders. Differences among the programs are based on the terrain and type of operations that first responders will undertake. All training programs teach the same basic concepts.

URBAN SEARCH AND RESCUE

The Federal Emergency Management Agency (FEMA), part of the U.S. Department of Homeland Security, provides urban search-and-rescue training. FEMA's urban search and rescue (US&R) program is stringent. The training prepares candidates for certification in the location, rescue, and initial medical stabilization of individuals trapped in confined spaces due to a structural collapse or other accident. Each trainee must be an EMT. There are hundreds of hours of additional training beyond the EMT level. FEMA provides the training directly to those seeking certification. The training is dangerous, as trainees receive instruction for situations involving structural collapse. There is also training for medical specialists and logistics specialists. Specialties such as canine (K-9) search have additional training requirements.

WILDERNESS SEARCH AND RESCUE

The National Association for Search & Rescue provides training and certification at a number of different levels. The most basic level of training is provided in NASAR's Introduction to Search and Rescue (ISAR). This training prepares candidates for certification at the level known as SARTECH III. Students learn about the overall responsibilities, skills, abilities, and

Swiftwater search and rescue requires the proper clothing and equipment for responders. Rescuers must also practice using the force of the water to help in their efforts.

equipment needed for a search-and-rescue mission with emphasis on the wilderness aspect of the work. Students learn about search-and-rescue operations while learning to use a compass and a topographical map, along with the specific techniques that wilderness searchers use.

The next level of training is NASAR's Fundamentals of Search and Rescue (FUNSAR). It covers general responsibilities and includes a practice mission in which students put their skills to the test. The right equipment and clothing is necessary for FUNSAR training. Total FUNSAR training time is forty-seven hours, held for five days straight or over two weekends. At the end of training, the candidate is ready to take the SARTECH II certification exam.

SARTECH I/Crew Leader is the advanced level of SAR training. It is intended for people who serve as field searchers or crew leaders on search-and-rescue missions. NASAR also offers canine SARTECH training.

SWIFTWATER SEARCH AND RESCUE

Swiftwater rescue training includes the basics of any first responder training and then adds a twist—having to do it all while soaking wet and struggling against strong currents. In this type of search and rescue, the injured are at risk not only from their injuries, but also from the water and water temperature. A basic component of swiftwater training is learning to use the force of the moving water to assist in the rescue. The proper use of ropes and other equipment is also essential in this type of rescue.

The required skills for surface and swiftwater rescue in the United States and Canada are based on National Fire Protection Association (NFPA) standards. According to NFPA 1006 (*Professional Qualifications for Rescue Technicians*, 2008 edition), there are two levels of qualification. The first is a Level 1 Rescuer. The more advanced is a Level 2 Rescuer. The Rescuer is capable of more advanced technical rescue operations. There are also ratings for specialties such as surf rescue, ice rescue, and dive rescue.

A U.S. Coast Guard helicopter and crew perform a rescue after Hurricane Katrina in New Orleans, Louisiana, in 2005. The U.S. Coast Guard provides training to a variety of agencies and volunteers.

COAST GUARD SEARCH AND RESCUE

The U.S. Coast Guard provides training to U.S. Coast Guard personnel—active-duty members, reservists, civilians, and auxiliarists. U.S. Coast Guard personnel and other first responders who work on the waterways use cutters, other boats, and aircraft to complete their missions. The National Search and Rescue School is a joint coast guard/air force program that trains candidates in oceanic, coastal, and inland search techniques. The program teaches trainees to aid persons in distress and bring them to safety while respecting the safety of the crew. The U.S. Coast Guard is the Maritime Search and Rescue Coordinator for the United States under the National SAR Plan. The air force is responsible for inland search and rescue.

To ensure it has the equipment and personnel available when and where needed, the U.S. Coast Guard has SAR facilities on the East, West, and Gulf coasts. It also has facilities on the Great Lakes and inland waterways, as well as in Alaska, Hawaii, Guam, and Puerto Rico. Training at the National Search and Rescue School is available to SAR professionals from all U.S. military branches, various U.S. government agencies, volunteer SAR organizations, and members of the international SAR community.

CANINE SEARCH AND RESCUE

There are many levels of search-and-rescue training for canine teams. They include four levels of trailing search certification in which the dog and trainer track and locate a single stationary object in a wilderness environment. The team must also trail and locate a stationary subject in an urban environment. In addition, there are three levels of certification for an area search in which the dog and handler must locate a single stationary subject in a predefined area without a GPS. The criteria for these levels of certification include an assessment of the handler's skills, the dog's skills, and the handler and

A successful canine team consists of an experienced human handler and a well-trained dog. Additional training is needed for this highly specialized work.

dog's team skills. To be successful in canine SAR, handlers must have good land navigation field skills and work well with their dog. Specialty training for canine SAR in avalanche and human remains detection is also available.

USAR TASK FORCES

Members of urban search-and-rescue task forces such as VA-TF1 and CA-TF2 have an even greater training burden. They must be capable of arriving at a natural or manmade disaster with all the equipment that they will need to be self-sufficient as they race to locate and free the injured from structural collapses and other small spaces. They must be able to do this while tremors are ongoing, or the threat of additional high water or severe weather is imminent.

Training is ongoing for task force members. Many are required to train monthly to maintain their skills. They are not paid for this training time. Members of the team are certified EMTs and paramedics, as well as civilian doctors, canine handlers, structural engineers, communications specialists, and heavy rigging specialists. The EMTs, paramedics, and communications specialists in VA-TF1 and CA-TF2 are part of the Fairfax County Fire and Rescue Department and the Los Angeles County Fire Department, respectively. Many of the task force members have received advanced training in specialty areas such as hazardous materials, swiftwater rescue, and weapons of mass destruction awareness.

chapter 3

GETTING A FIRST JOB AS A FIRST RESPONDER

L anding the first job in any profession can be a challenge. Getting a first job as a first responder requires some planning and creativity on the candidate's part.

FIRST STEPS

A useful first step in exploring careers as a first responder is to read the information available about the skills needed for certification. It's also a good idea to take a CPR (cardiopulmonary resuscitation) or first-aid course while still in high school. These skills will provide a sound base for the additional training that will be required. Training classes in first aid and CPR also give candidates the opportunity to see if emergency response work is a good fit. The American Red Cross offers training in first aid, CPR, and AED (automated external defibrillator). They also hold courses on wilderness and remote first aid, sports safety training, and pet first aid. In many cases, successful completion of courses leads to certifications in those skills. These certifications are useful to have when applying for a first job as a first responder.

To try out their future role and gain some experience, candidates can also volunteer as health aides at a summer camp or other organization. The fact that a candidate can demonstrate an active interest in the career field will make a difference when applying for that first job. Once candidates have completed a first-aid class, they can volunteer to present those skills to others, for example, assisting local youth organizations that have merit badges in first aid. Thinking of creative ways to show potential employers your dedication to the career field is one way that successful candidates stand out from the rest.

Since there are many different types of first responders, deciding upon the type of work that fits one's personality and interests is important. Researching the positions available and the paying status of those jobs is another important step. Since EMTs, paramedics, urban and wilderness SAR professionals, canine teams, and swiftwater first responders perform their duties in different environments, it helps if candidates focus on organizations or regions that are most likely to offer positions in their area of interest. For example, national parks

Taking CPR and first-aid classes is a good start for teens considering careers as first responders. The skills taught are important and provide a first look at the field.

or areas with significant acreage of mountains will likely have active wilderness search-and-rescue teams. Areas with rivers that attract recreational users will likely have swiftwater search-and-rescue teams.

COURSEWORK AFTER HIGH SCHOOL

Many community and four-year colleges offer coursework for first responders. The courses may be part of the training required by a specific rescue company for a specific position. It is also possible to take coursework in preparation for certification without having a specific open position in mind. Candidates with a paid position requiring basic EMT training are often paid at an hourly rate. Those with advanced EMT certification will make an annual salary, and paramedics will make even more.

Since many first responder jobs are volunteer positions, candidates who are hired for these positions typically have paying jobs, too. It's possible that a candidate will work in an area that has little to do with his or her responsibilities as a first responder, but it is more likely that the paying position will be in a field that's closely related. Some possibilities include jobs in communications, security, or with a private ambulance service, in which key skills and physical conditioning will be put to use and encouraged.

APPLYING FOR THE JOB

Once a candidate identifies organizations that handle the type of work that he or she wants to do, applying for jobs is the next step. Sometimes there won't be any jobs listed, or a candidate will be unable to find a complete listing. When that happens, a letter of introduction can start the process. In the letter of introduction, candidates explain their interest in the type

Coursework for first responder certification is offered at many community colleges. On-the-job training may be available through apprenticeships, volunteer positions, or internships.

of first responder work performed by that organization. They explain why they are a good fit for the job and include any classes, volunteer positions, or clubs that demonstrate their interest. They close by asking to be considered for any present or future openings. They may also add that they'd appreciate a meeting to get advice as to how to go about getting a first responder position.

If there is a publicized open position, candidates apply directly for that position. When filling in the application, remember that it's important to:

- Fill in any paperwork neatly and thoroughly. This paperwork is the first introduction a candidate has to an organization.
- Write in ink or type. Bring a black or blue pen along if you will be filling out paperwork in person.
- Take the time to write a thoughtful reply to any questions that require several sentences as an answer.

Remember that it is important for candidates to match their experience to the questions on the application. Any volunteer work or first-aid classes will help make some candidates more attractive than others.

There may be an apprenticeship program for first responders in a candidate's area of interest. The Department of Labor has listings of the vocations that have active apprenticeship programs. Entering an apprenticeship program is a serious step. A candidate is agreeing to complete training that may take up to two years, often without pay. At the end of the apprenticeship, the candidate will be rewarded either with certification that will lead to a job or with an actual job.

A candidate can also call local first responder organizations and ask if there are training programs or volunteer positions available. It's important for candidates to plan out the first few calls, even practicing what they will say. At the very least, candidates need to introduce themselves, explain that they are interested in a career as a first responder, and tell the contact about any training or certification they have. Then they can follow up by saying that they are interested in any opportunity to learn the skills they'll need for a career as a first responder.

THE INTERVIEW

Interviews can be stressful. Candidates want to make a good first impression. The people conducting the interviews want to fill the position with the best possible candidate. During an interview, it's important for candidates to be comfortable with themselves and follow these simple tips:

- Make a positive first impression by dressing appropriately for the interview. Candidates can ask a guidance counselor for advice if they are unsure what is appropriate for a particular interview.
- A candidate should introduce himself or herself and shake hands firmly with the interviewer before the interview begins.
- Make eye contact and speak clearly. This is not the time to mumble or appear distracted.
- Request clarification if a question is confusing.
- Don't be afraid to ask for the job at the end of the interview. At the very least, convey your enthusiasm and ask what the next step will be.

It's a good idea to prepare for the interview by anticipating the types of questions that will be asked. Candidates should be prepared to state why a career as a first responder is of interest. They should also be able to describe any classes they have taken or actual experience they have. If asked what makes him or her

MATCHING YOUR QUALIFICATIONS TO THE JOB

Rom Duckworth, a nationally recognized emergency services lecturer, gave a presentation as part of the Danbury Ambulance Service Education and Career Development Program in Danbury, Connecticut. He offers some advice to job seekers preparing to interview for first responder positions.

"Every answer that comes out of your mouth should connect you with that job," he says. "No matter what they're asking, you need to show how you are the right candidate. The best. The right fit for the job in every single answer that you give."

To accomplish this, take some time to think about the requirements for an EMS position and the experience you have both in and out of the classroom. Making a list of skills and responsibilities—and then matching your experiences to these requirements—will help you show why you are the right person for the job. It can be as simple as demonstrating that you are cool in an emergency because of the work you did with young day campers. It can be as specific as describing the care you provided to a sick relative. It might even be pointing out that your role as captain of a successful athletic team gave you the skills to lead others effectively.

Duckworth explains that it is important to back up your assertions about yourself with specific examples like these. Instead of simply calling yourself a "people person," Duckworth recommends giving an example of a past job in which you worked with challenging customers successfully. He suggests saying, "Because I was the best at dealing with the most difficult people, I was always the person who was called upon to deal with the difficult people. I was always dealing with the most difficult, and I still enjoyed the job."

Duckworth believes that starting to build a résumé is a useful exercise, since it requires you to generate examples of your past achievements and positive qualities. Duckworth says you should "start coming up with your own specific examples where you have shown, where you have demonstrated, where you have proven all of the personal qualities about yourself that you're then going to connect with the department."

uniquely qualified for the job, a candidate might talk about his or her successes working with others or the ability to communicate well.

It is common for an interviewer to ask a candidate about his or her greatest success or regret. When talking about a success or an achievement, an example of a way in which the candidate solved a problem or worked successfully with a team is ideal. If asked about a regret, a candidate can frame a positive reply by adding what he or she would do differently with the insight and maturity he or she now possesses.

PROBATIONARY OR TRAINING PERIOD

Since so many first responders work as part of a team, it is possible that a candidate will have a probationary or training period with the team at first. During this time, the candidate is evaluated to see if he or she is a good fit for the team. The candidate also has the chance to demonstrate his or her skills and see if the team is one that he or she would like to work with.

A probationary or training period is an important time for the candidate to:

- Demonstrate a positive attitude.
- Experience the actual requirements of the job.
- Ask questions and observe procedures.

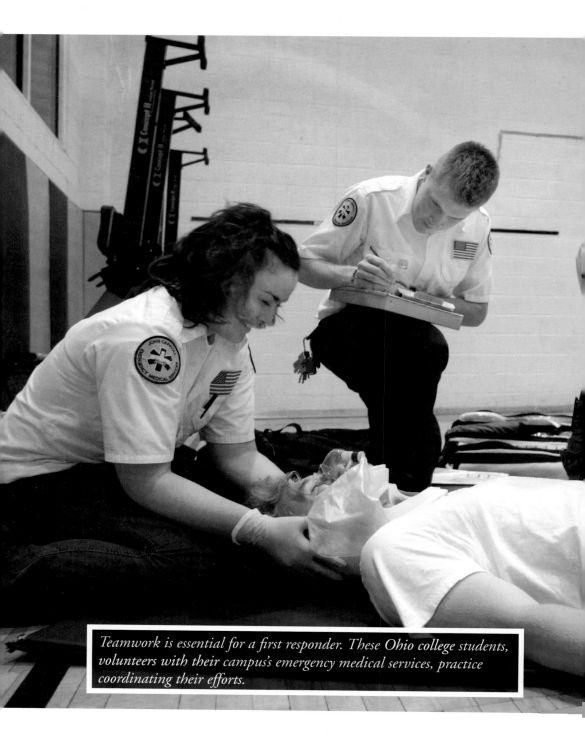

Teamwork is essential for a first responder. These Ohio college students, volunteers with their campus's emergency medical services, practice coordinating their efforts.

- Observe experienced professionals as they carry out their duties.
- Prove he or she will be a positive addition to the team.

It's important for a candidate to appreciate the advantages of a probationary or training period. It provides the opportunity to get an inside look at the team and organization before making a final commitment.

VOLUNTEERING TO GAIN EXPERIENCE

It's possible there will not be an open position when a candidate is ready for a first job as a first responder. It's also possible the position a candidate wants will require more hands-on experience than the candidate possesses. When that is the case, one solution is to volunteer with organizations doing the type of first responder work a candidate desires.

For a candidate interested in urban, wilderness, or swiftwater search-and-rescue work, this may mean seeking a position that does not require the most advanced training but will provide him or her with real-world experience by being part of the team. Such a volunteer position will demonstrate the candidate's commitment to the career field as the candidate gains experience and qualifies for each level of certification.

chapter 4

FROM JOBS TO CAREERS

J ust what does a career as a first responder look like? What sorts of positions will a first responder hold? What responsibilities will he or she have? Can training as a first responder lead to other opportunities in the health care field? What is the career path for a first responder?

Because there are so many different types of first responders, there is not one answer to these questions. For example, EMTs and paramedics are employed by private ambulance companies as well as by municipalities. The position, responsibilities, and hours will depend upon the type of emergency response work a candidate decides to do. In addition, as a first responder's experience increases, new opportunities may arise. For example, advanced-level EMTs, paramedics, and SAR professionals have the option of becoming instructors.

Despite the many differences in emergency response careers, there are some things that all first responder careers have in common.

DAILY LIFE ON THE JOB

From the early days of the militia and the very first fire departments, first responders have been part of a long tradition of volunteer service to the community. That means that, in many cases, a first responder is not working in a paid position. However, as urban areas grow, the population ages, and the need for EMTs and paramedics becomes greater, there will likely be a greater number of paid positions. Paid or not, the requirements for these positions are rigorous, and the responsibilities are tremendous. First responders are literally responsible for the lives of others.

First responders often work in shifts. During those shifts, they may live at the firehouse or base for several days in a row. They are given a place to sleep and a locker for their things. They eat meals with the other volunteers as they wait for an emergency call. Once the call comes in, they will race to that location and spend as much or as little time as required to deal with the situation.

While first responders are waiting at the firehouse or station, a significant part of their time is spent maintaining the equipment used in operations. It's imperative that each piece of equipment work as intended when it is needed. There's no

First responders may spend many hours at the firehouse or station. Between calls, they train, inspect equipment, and share meals.

time in an emergency to hunt for a piece of equipment or get a broken piece of equipment to function properly.

Practice drills are another important part of the job of a first responder. While waiting for a call, the team will often hold practice drills to be certain all members can perform their duties quickly and properly. They also receive training and refresher courses to be certain they are prepared to carry out their duties without hesitation.

Because so much of a first responder's time on the job is spent with his or her team, and because so much of emergency response work depends upon good teamwork, it's important for first responders to work well with team members. It's also important for a first responder to be able to cooperate with other teams if the need arises. The common goal of all first responders is to reach the injured safely and quickly and then stabilize them for transport to a medical facility. All efforts are focused on that goal.

Practice drills are an important part of training. Here, a paramedic attends to actors pretending to be citizens injured in a terrorist explosion.

CAREERS FOR EMTS AND PARAMEDICS

A career as an EMT or paramedic differs based on a person's credentials. Certifications at different levels allow a first responder to perform different functions. EMTs are often broken into the following three categories:

(1) **EMT or EMT-Basic.** These professionals are certified to perform basic cardiac, respiratory, and traumatic injury emergency care. These are the professionals who stabilize the injured and then care for patients on the way to the medical facility. They arrive at the scene of an accident or illness, park the ambulance in a safe location, assess the condition of the patient, obtain any background information available, stabilize the patient, and transport that patient to the medical facility. At the medical facility, they complete any required reports and brief the ER personnel on the patient's condition.

(2) **EMT-Intermediate or Advanced EMT.** Advanced emergency medical technicians are certified to provide both basic and advanced life support. They are trained in the use of defibrillators, intubation, administration of IV fluids, and other advanced techniques to monitor heart activity. They also transport the patient to a medical facility, file required reports, and brief ER personnel on the patient's condition. Their level of responsibility and certified abilities are greater than an EMT because of the additional hours of training.

(3) **Paramedic or EMT-P.** These professionals have the most advanced level of certification and usually hold paying positions. They are cleared to administer oral and IV medication. They can also intubate patients or perform surgical airway insertion when required. They can place central venous lines when necessary or use mechanical ventilation to assist

With higher levels of training and experience come increased responsibility. These paramedics are certified to administer IV medication to the injured.

respiratory function. They transport the patient to the medical facility, file required reports, and brief ER personnel on the patient's condition. They are the most highly trained EMTs and typically hold two-year degrees or have completed an apprentice program.

Another career option for a trained EMT or paramedic is to become an EMT dispatcher/scheduler. Professionals in this position are responsible for taking service requests and scheduling and dispatching the proper resources. They are responsible for ensuring that the necessary equipment reaches the injured person as quickly as possible. Individuals in this position need good communication skills. They must have the ability to work well under stress and keep track of multiple priorities.

In addition, those with EMT or paramedic training often continue their career with work in other areas of health care. Many EMTs go on to earn degrees in medical fields. They may become nurses or doctors. They may choose to work in emergency departments or in trauma care. The time spent as an EMT makes them attractive candidates for medical schools. It also gives candidates an opportunity to be certain that this stressful but rewarding career path is right for them.

Some former EMTs and paramedics work for hospitals or other health care organizations as directors of emergency services. They work to ensure that the emergency services department of the organization is able to meet the needs of the patients served. The professional in this position may also be responsible for several emergency departments within a wider system. It is up to the director to make sure that resources are available when they are needed, where they are needed. Directors may also be responsible for preparing budgets and overseeing the management and development of key personnel. Many of these positions require a bachelor's or master's degree in nursing.

CAREERS IN SEARCH AND RESCUE

The National Association for Search & Rescue (NASAR) also has different levels of certification for search-and-rescue personnel. The work may be performed in an urban, wilderness, or swiftwater setting. It may involve work with canines or special equipment, such as helicopters. As with most career paths, the more experience and training an individual has, the more responsibility he or she will qualify for and the higher salary he or she will earn. NASAR's ranks include:

(1) **SARTECH III.** These professionals have completed training in the basics of search and rescue in rural and wilderness areas. They are able to assist in search-and-rescue operations, but they have no first-aid or other forms of life-saving training.

All search-and-rescue professionals must have strong field navigation skills. They must also be able to carry heavy packs and perform well outdoors under any conditions.

(2) **SARTECH II/FUNSAR.** Search-and-rescue professionals with this level of certification are able to take on broader job responsibilities. They can navigate during the day or night using a map and compass. They are versed in survival skills, facile with the use of a map, and able to track people who are lost. They are trained in the treatment of common medical emergencies and can explain why some types of equipment are better suited to a specific search than others. SAR personnel with this certification often assist with emergency medical care. They may also be managers of emergency response organizations.

(3) **SARTECH I/Crew Leader.** This is the most advanced level of certification for search and rescue personnel. Professionals with this level of training act as field searchers or

The twenty-four-hour ready pack includes first-aid and survival supplies like candles and antihistamines. It also includes gloves, extra clothing, and insect repellent. Optional items include goggles and a GPS.

What's in That Pack?

By the time individuals attain SAR I or crew leader certification, they must be ready to go at a moment's notice. To be certain of this, they have a twenty-four-hour ready pack standing by. It includes first-aid and survival supplies for the leader and crew. Here's a peek at some of the things on the packing list, adapted with permission from the National Association for Search & Rescue.

Personal/Crew First-Aid and Survival Kit

10 - Antacid tablets
10 - Antihistamine, 25 mg Benadryl
6 - Antiseptic cleansing pads
1 - Candle, long-burning
2 - Quarters, for phone call
16 - Matches in waterproof container
1 - Space-type blanket or sleeping bag
10 - Water purification tabs in sealed container or commercially approved purification device
1 - Whistle

Personal/SAR Crew Equipment

1 - Pack, adequate to carry required equipment
4 - Bags, various sizes, zip lock
1 - Cap or other headgear
1 - Clothing, extra set, suitable for climate
1 - Compass, orienteering
1 - Grid reader (UTM)
1 - Gloves, leather palm
1 - Insect repellent
1 - Knife, multipurpose
1 - Lip balm, with sunscreen
1 - Measuring device, 18 inches (.46 meters) minimum

1 - Metal cup or pot
1 - Mirror, small
1 - Nylon twine or small rope, 50 feet (50.24 m)
1 - Pace counter
1 - Pad and pencil
1 - Shelter material, 8 x 10 feet (2.44 x 3.05 m) plastic or coated nylon
1 - Watch

Optional Personal Equipment

1 - Altimeter
1 - Binoculars
1 - Foam pad
2 - Food, nonperishable
1 - Gaiters
1 - Goggles, clear
1 - Rain cover, pack
1 - Sunglasses, 97 percent UV protection
1 - Trail snacks
1 - Protractor
1- Handheld GPS (SAR appropriate) with two sets of extra batteries

crew leaders on SAR missions. These professionals have demonstrated that they can transport patients from the injury site using an improvised stretcher. They have received training in working with helicopters and searching in hazardous terrain. They also have at least a current Advanced First Aid certification as well as a current CPR certification. It is more likely that someone in this position will be an EMT or even a paramedic. They also have at least two years of active membership with a SAR organization and over one hundred hours of SAR training.

CAREER AS A TASK FORCE MEMBER

Members of urban search-and-rescue task forces such as VA-TF1 and CA-TF2, are among the most highly trained and qualified search-and-rescue professionals in the world. They work with local companies until called upon to travel to the site of a man-made or natural disaster. They can be called upon at any time, must be ready to travel immediately, and must be able to go away for up to fourteen days at a time. They must be physically fit and prepared to deal with whatever they find upon arrival.

The teams are designed to be completely self-sufficient. This means that they bring in all the equipment required to meet their needs. In this way, they do not become an additional burden on already stretched resources in a disaster area. They are professionals, dedicated to searching and extricating individuals who are in the most urgent need of care in situations in which there are scant resources.

chapter 5

BENEFITS, RISKS, AND OUTLOOK FOR FIRST RESPONDERS

For many, the best part of the job of a first responder is the satisfaction that comes from knowing they've helped to save lives. There is also the excitement that comes with the urgency of the situation and the need to think quickly in an emergency. For someone who enjoys working closely with others and thrives on the challenge of testing one's skills in a variety of different situations, a career as a first responder is just right.

BENEFITS AND HOURS

Benefits for first responders vary widely depending upon the employer, but they can be quite generous. They often include paid vacation; sick leave; retirement plans; and medical, dental, and vision insurance. Some employers also provide life insurance and on-site childcare. In the large city of New York,

First responders work with people during a difficult time. The ability to get the job done while being reassuring and calm is an important part of the career.

AN INSIDE LOOK AT THE WORLD'S LARGEST EMS COMMAND

The EMTs and paramedics employed by the Fire Department of New York (FDNY) are part of the largest emergency service in the world. Members of the FDNY EMS Command earn a base salary with yearly increases. In addition to the base salary, these first responders earn overtime, shift differentials, meal money, and other benefits. Here are some additional details:

- Positions in the FDNY EMS Command are full-time.
- EMS members respond to about 3,000 emergencies a day and nearly 1.2 million medical emergencies each year.
- Their response time is at historic lows throughout the five boroughs.
- EMS Command provides some of the most advanced prehospital medical care anywhere in the world.
- EMTs provide basic life support (BLS) services ranging from CPR to spinal immobilization.
- Paramedics provide advanced life support (ALS) services ranging from some invasive procedures to dispensing medications under the supervision of a physician.
- Paramedics and EMTs can become lieutenants, captains, chiefs, or even firefighters.
- All training materials are provided free of charge as long as the candidate is an active FDNY EMS member.

The first step? Take the Emergency Medical Specialist EMT Exam (Exam #2004) during the open competitive exam period.

benefits for EMS members of the fire department include three weeks' vacation to start. Pension benefits include vesting after five years and a full pension after twenty-five years of service, regardless of age. There is also money paid for overtime, shift differentials, and for meals, as well as programs that provide tax benefits to employees, such as deferred compensation and flexible spending accounts for health care.

There are also emotional benefits for first responders. They have the satisfaction of knowing they have helped people in very difficult circumstances. Their careers include work with the injured and ill, young and old, with satisfactory outcomes for many. Unfortunately, some outcomes will not be positive. The first responder has to be able to deal with that, too.

Depending on the organization for which a first responder works, on the job hours can range from a standard workweek to shift work that can span weekends, or a forty-eight-hour shift, followed by several days off. There is no expectation that a first responder will have weekends or holidays off. These professionals are often on call during evenings, weekends, and holidays.

RISKS

The role of a first responder is a risky one. These professionals respond to emergencies without full knowledge of the circumstances they will find. They must be physically fit so that they can lift and bend to provide care to the ill and the injured. They must be able to work well under a variety of conditions, including the scenes of traffic accidents, fires, and natural disasters. They must be prepared to calm the injured while dealing with bystanders and onlookers who are also reacting emotionally to the events as they occur. First responders must also be prepared to face injury themselves, even though they are trained to drive at high speeds and proceed in the safest way possible to avoid injury to themselves and further injury to patients.

Emotional burnout is a risk for first responders. They see adults and children in pain and difficult situations on a regular basis. They are involved in some of the most challenging moments of the injured person's life. The stress level is high. First responders must not only reach the accident scene quickly and without incident, but also remain cool and reassuring as they perform their duties, often under difficult circumstances. All of this can take a toll on a first responder.

GENERAL OUTLOOK

As the population of the United States ages and metropolitan areas grow, the need for first responders will also grow. Whether it is for private ambulance services or municipal departments, first responders

Members of Oklahoma Task Force 1 search the rubble after the tornado in Joplin, Missouri. First responders must be ready to go to work, even in dangerous conditions.

like EMTs and paramedics will be in increased demand. For the nation as a whole, the U.S. Department of Labor's Bureau of Labor Statistics anticipates a 9 percent increase in the number of EMTs and paramedics, from 210,700 in 2008 to a projected 229,700 in 2018. The area with the most growth is projected to be ambulance services.

Increased use of national parks and other recreation areas is likely to support an increase in the demand for search-and-rescue professionals. Many of these positions will remain volunteer in nature. Individuals filling these positions will come from a variety of professions. Volunteers will be drawn to SAR work because of their love of the outdoors and the opportunity to work with a team and put their training to practical use.

Rural areas will have a greater need for EMS professionals as the population ages. Depending on the demographics of an area, positions may be volunteer jobs, rather than paid

First responders in New York City care for an injured cyclist who must be transported to the hospital in an ambulance.

ones. The need for these professionals will be urgent either way. In areas where emergency professionals are volunteers, it is likely that local employers will work with EMTs and paramedics to accommodate their schedules. Because rural communities are often far from medical facilities, certified first responders

Private ambulance crews assist in the evacuation of a hospital in a low-lying part of New York in preparation for Hurricane Irene in 2011.

play a critical role in the health care delivery systems of these areas. It is also possible that more positions will become paid positions as the need for EMS professionals becomes greater than what the community can provide through the services of volunteers.

Many urban areas already have EMS services with paid, rather than volunteer, positions. This is because the demand for these services is so great that a network of volunteers would not be capable of meeting the demand effectively and efficiently. With paid positions and benefits, the competition is tough. Candidates may have to wait months or longer for a position to open up. Candidates who are certified paramedics will likely have less difficulty finding a position, since they are in the highest demand.

Private ambulance services help meet the needs of populations residing in elder communities and assisted living homes as well as seniors with known, preexisting conditions who need emergency transport to a medical facility. As the American population ages, there will be more of these jobs for EMTs and paramedics. As with the paid positions in urban areas, the competition for these positions will likely be tough. It will be important for candidates to be in peak physical condition and thoroughly trained to earn one of these positions.

For some employers, it makes sense to contract with private companies in order to have professionals who are trained and ready to meet the emergency needs of their employees. It may be a biotech firm that wants to ensure a swift response in the event of a lab incident or a manufacturing facility that wants to ensure its workers have a response time that is even lower than that possible with the existing EMS service in the area.

THE BUREAU OF LABOR STATISTICS OUTLOOK

As mentioned previously, the Bureau of Labor Statistics projects that in the ten-year period from 2008 to 2018, there will be a 9 percent increase in the total number of EMTs and paramedics employed. It based this rate of growth in large part on the rising call volume caused by an aging population. Adding to the need for EMTs and paramedics is the fact that emergency departments across the country are increasingly overcrowded. Because of this, some ambulances are directed to less crowded emergency rooms, requiring EMS personnel to spend more time with patients. Also, crowded emergency rooms may not be able to take a patient immediately, so the EMS crew will spend additional time with that patient as well. The increasing aging population combined with overcrowded emergency facilities will likely result in the need for more crews and equipment.

Another factor cited by the Bureau of Labor Statistics is the growing number of medical facilities that specialize in a particular type of treatment. Because this is the case, it may be better for the patient to travel a bit farther to reach a medical facility that is better equipped to handle that patient's needs. This additional travel results in a longer time spent with the patient and a need for more EMS personnel.

The Bureau of Labor Statistics anticipates a trend toward paid EMS positions. This is because of the large amount of training and serious time commitment these positions require. The competition for jobs with local government and third-service rescue squads will be greatest because of the better salaries and benefits. Those with advanced education and certification will be best positioned to get jobs and offer the highest levels of pre-hospital care.

Earnings vary widely, according to the employment situation and geographic location of EMT and paramedic jobs. The amount of training and experience that an EMT or paramedic has also plays a role in compensation, according to the Bureau of Labor Statistics. For median hourly wages, consult the most recent edition of the bureau's *Occupational Outlook Handbook*. With the great range in salaries, it is up to the

EMT or paramedic to factor in other aspects of a job when deciding where to work. Some of those might be the hours, number of calls per shift, length of shifts, recreational and cultural advantages of a location, and other personal considerations.

The job of a first responder is not for everyone. Hours are long and conditions can be stressful. Training is rigorous and standards are high. That's because first responders are the ones who reach those in need first and care for them until they can reach a medical facility. As a result, those who decide upon careers as first responders not only earn good salaries and receive excellent benefits, but also have the satisfaction of knowing they are saving lives.

glossary

AED Automated external defibrillator; a portable electronic device that automatically diagnoses cardiac arrhythmias and treats them through defibrillation.

backboard A stiff board on which an injured person, especially one with suspected neck or spinal injuries, is placed in order to immobilize the person and prevent further injury during travel.

backcountry A remote rural area.

certified first responder An individual who is trained and certified to render emergency prehospital medical attention to the injured at the scene of an accident or disaster.

coordinator A person who oversees all the parts of the operation and decides upon the role of each person.

CPR Cardiopulmonary resuscitation; a life-saving technique used when breathing or heartbeat has stopped. It includes rescue breathing and chest compressions.

defibrillate To stop uncoordinated contractions of the heart.

deploy To put into action.

EKG Electrocardiogram; a printed recording of the electrical activity of the heart.

en route On or along the way.

extricate To free or remove from an entanglement or difficulty.

GPS Global positioning system; a navigation system that uses satellite signals to find the location of a radio receiver.

imminent Likely to occur at any moment.

immobilize To prevent or restrict normal movement; fix in place.

inclement Severe or stormy.

intubation The insertion of a tube into a hollow organ (such as the trachea) to maintain an open airway, allow drainage, or administer anesthetics or oxygen.

recovery Retrieving the remains of the deceased.

swiftwater rescue A rescue discipline that deals with rescue and recovery from rapidly moving water.

vital signs Signs monitored by a health professional to check a person's level of physical functioning. Vital signs include heartbeat/pulse, breathing rate, blood pressure, and temperature.

for more information

Coast Guard Training Center Yorktown
Commanding Officer
1 U.S. Coast Guard Training Center
Yorktown, VA 23690
(757) 856-2000
Web site: http://www.uscg.mil/tcyorktown/Ops/SAR/default.asp
The Coast Guard Training Center Yorktown offers search-
and-rescue training to coast guard and other armed
services personnel, state and federal agencies, and personnel from allied nations.

Federal Emergency Management Agency (FEMA)
U.S. Department of Homeland Security
500 C Street SW
Washington, DC 20472
(202) 646-2500
Web site: http://www.fema.gov
FEMA established the Urban Search and Rescue (US&R)
Response System in 1989. It provides the structure for the
coordination of local emergency services personnel in the
event of a disaster.

Government of Canada National Search and Rescue Secretariat
Canadian Beacon Registry
CFB Trenton
P.O. Box 1000 Stn Forces
Astra, ON K0K 3W0
Canada
(877) 406-SOS1 [7671]
Web site: http://www.nss.gc.ca

The National Search and Rescue Secretariat is responsible for the management and coordination of the Canadian National Search and Rescue (SAR) Program.

National Association of Emergency Medical Technicians (NAEMT)
132-A East Northside Drive
Clinton, MS 39060-1400
(601) 924-7744
Web site: http://www.naemt.org
The NAEMT represents and serves emergency medical services personnel by providing education, membership, and advocacy at the national level.

National Association for Search & Rescue (NASAR)
P.O. Box 232020
Centreville, VA 20120
(703) 222-6277
Web site: http://www.nasar.org
The NASAR prepares individuals for search-and-rescue operations. It offers training and certification classes and conferences.

National Registry of Emergency Medical Technicians (NREMT)
Rocco V. Morando Building
6610 Busch Boulevard
P.O. Box 29233
Columbus, OH 43229
(614) 888-4484
Web site: http://www.nremt.org
Founded in 1970 at the recommendation of the Committee on Highway Traffic Safety, the NREMT sets uniform standards for training and examination of individuals engaged in the delivery of emergency ambulance service.

Paramedic Association of Canada
201-4 Florence Street
Ottawa, ON K2P 0W7
Canada
(613) 836-6581
Web site: http://paramedic.ca
Located in Ontario, Canada, the Paramedic Association of
    Canada is a voluntary professional association for para-
    medical personnel.

Whitewater Rescue Institute (WRI)
210 Red Fox Road
Lolo, MT 59847
(406) 207-2027
Web site: http://www.whitewaterrescue.com
The WRI offers national and international swiftwater and
    wilderness medicine training courses.

WEB SITES

Due to the changing nature of Internet links, Rosen Publishing
has developed an online list of Web sites related to the subject
of this book. This site is updated regularly. Please use this link
to access the list:

http://www.rosenlinks.com/ECAR/FRepo

for further reading

Aehlert, Barbara. *Emergency Medical Responder: First Responder in Action.* 2nd ed. New York, NY: McGraw-Hill, 2011.

Bergeron, J. David, Chris Le Baudour, Gloria Bizjak, and Keith Wesley. *First Responder.* 8th ed. Upper Saddle River, NJ: Pearson/Prentice Hall, 2009.

Chapleau, Will. *Emergency First Responder: Making the Difference.* 2nd ed. St. Louis, MO: MosbyJems/Elsevier, 2011.

Ferry, Monica. *Search and Rescue Specialist and Careers in FEMA* (Homeland Security and Counterterrorism Careers). Berkeley Heights, NJ: Enslow Publishers, 2006.

Haugen, Hayley Mitchell. *Disaster Relief* (Issues That Concern You). Detroit, MI: Greenhaven Press, 2010.

Limmer, Daniel, Keith J. Karren, Brent Q. Hafen, and Edward T. Dickinson. *First Responder: A Skills Approach.* 7th ed. Upper Saddle River, NJ: Pearson/Prentice Hall, 2007.

National Safety Council. *First Responder Pocket Guide.* Boston, MA: McGraw-Hill Higher Education, 2008.

Robson, David. *Disaster Response* (Compact Research Series). San Diego, CA: ReferencePoint Press, 2010.

Roza, Greg. *Disaster Relief Workers* (Extreme Careers). New York, NY: Rosen Publishing Group, 2007.

Schottke, David, and Andrew N. Pollak. *Emergency Medical Responder: Your First Response in Emergency Care.* 5th ed. Sudbury, MA: Jones & Bartlett Learning, 2011.

Tilton, Buck. *Wilderness First Responder: How to Recognize, Treat, and Prevent Emergencies in the Backcountry.* 3rd ed. Guilford, CT: FalconGuides, 2010.

Vernon, August. *First Responder Critical Incident Guide.* Chester, MD: Red Hat Publishing Company, 2009.

bibliography

American Red Cross. "First Aid/CPR/AED—More First Aid and CPR Topics." Retrieved November 22, 2011 (http://www.redcross.org).

American Red Cross. "Hurricane Recovery Program." Retrieved November 22, 2011 (http://www.redcross.org).

American Red Cross. "International Services." Retrieved November 22, 2011 (http://www.redcross.org).

DisasterDog.org. "HomePage." 2011. Retrieved January 27, 2012 (http://www.disasterdog.org).

EMT National Training – National Exams. "EMT B Practice Tests—Exam Questions." 2012. Retrieved January 27, 2012 (http://www.emt-national-training.com/practice_tests.php).

Federal Emergency Management Agency. "About US&R." August 11, 2010. Retrieved November 23, 2011 (http://www.fema.gov/emergency/usr/about.shtm).

Los Angeles County Fire Department. "Special Ops—Tech Ops—CA-TF2." 2005. Retrieved December 15, 2011 (http://fire.lacounty.gov/SpecialOps/TechOpsCA-TF2.asp).

Mountain Rescue Association. "Mountain Rescue Training Programs." Retrieved January 23, 2012 (http://www.mra.org/training/mountain-rescue-training).

National Association of Emergency Medical Technicians. "NAEMT—Education." 2008. Retrieved January 3, 2012 (http://www.naemt.org/education/education_home.aspx).

National Association for Search & Rescue. "Courses and Certifications." 2012. Retrieved May 1, 2012 (http://www.nasar.org/page/20/Courses-and-Certifications).

National Association for Search & Rescue. "Education." Retrieved January 10, 2012 (http://www.nasar.org/page/2/Education).

National Registry of Emergency Medical Technicians.
"National EMS Certification Examinations." 2012.
Retrieved January 15, 2012 (http://www.nremt.org).

New York City Fire Department. "FDNY EMS Benefits and
Salary." 2011. Retrieved February 2, 2012 (http://home2
.nyc.gov/html/fdny/html/community/ems_salary_benefits_
042607.shtml).

Rescue 3 International. "Rescue 3: List of Courses." 2010.
Retrieved January 15, 2012 (http://www.rescue3international
.com/courselist.php).

SectionHiker.com. "Search and Rescue Interview: Harrison
Ripps, CMSART." 2012. Retrieved February 2, 2012
(http://sectionhiker.com/search-and-rescue-interview-
harrison-ripps-cmsart).

U.S. Coast Guard, U.S. Department of Homeland Security.
"Overview." Retrieved November 22, 2011 (http://www
.uscg.mil/tcyorktown/Ops/SAR/default.asp).

U.S. Coast Guard, U.S. Department of Homeland Security.
"SAR Facts, Reports, Presentations & Info Sheets."
Retrieved November 22, 2011 (http://www.uscg.mil
/hq/cg5/cg534/SAR_facts_reports.asp).

U.S. Coast Guard, U.S. Department of Homeland Security.
"USCG: Careers." Retrieved November 22, 2011 (http://
www.uscg.mil/top/careers.asp).

U.S. Department of Labor, Bureau of Labor Statistics.
"Emergency Medical Technicians and Paramedics."
Occupational Outlook Handbook. 2010–11 ed. Retrieved
January 27, 2012 (http://www.bls.gov/oco/ocos101.htm).

U.S. Department of Labor, Bureau of Labor Statistics. "Fire
Fighters." *Occupational Outlook Handbook.* 2010–11 ed.
Retrieved January 27, 2012 (http://www.bls.gov/oco
/ocos329.htm).

U.S. Department of Labor, Employment and Training
Administration. "State Apprenticeship Information."

March 27, 2004. Retrieved January 21, 2012 (http://www
.doleta.gov/OA/sainformation.cfm).

Virginia Task Force 1, Fairfax County Urban Search and
Rescue. "About VA-TF1." 2012. Retrieved January 3,
2012 (http://www.vatf1.org).

Virginia Task Force 1, Fairfax County Urban Search and
Rescue. "Family Support." 2011. Retrieved November 30,
2011 (http://www.vatf1.org).

Whitewater Rescue Institute. "Water Training Courses."
2011. Retrieved December 17, 2011 (http://www
.whitewaterrescue.com/courses/water).

Whitewater Rescue Institute. "Wilderness Medicine Courses."
2011. Retrieved December 17, 2011 (http://www
.whitewaterrescue.com/courses/wilderness-medicine).

YouTube.com. "Emergency Medical Technician (EMT)
Interview with Tim Moyer." January 21, 2010. Retrieved
February 2, 2012 (http://youtu.be/rUvQ5XanFbY).

YouTube.com. "EMS Week 2011 Paramedic Interview." May
17, 2011. Retrieved February 2, 2012 (http://www
.youtube.com/watch?v=3IORpIKEcTY&feature=youtu.be).

YouTube.com. "Fairfax County Urban Search & Rescue Team
Mobilizes to Japan." March 11, 2011. Retrieved February
2, 2012 (http://youtu.be/67f4VTMgM80).

YouTube.com. "How to Interview for Fire and EMS." March
11, 2011. Retrieved February 2, 2012 (http://youtu.be/
qDGd4wjsVJM).

index

ABOUT THE AUTHOR

Gina Hagler is an award-winning published author. She is a member of the Society of Children's Book Writers and Illustrators and the American Society of Journalists and Authors. She writes on a variety of topics for children and adults. She often writes about the day-to-day work of scientists and other professionals.

PHOTO CREDITS

Cover (paramedic), pp. 56–57 Tyler Olson/Shutterstock.com; cover (background), pp. 1, 18–19, 22–23, 30, 42–43, 45 © AP Images; pp. 4, 17, 32–33 Nicholas Kamm/AFP/Getty Images; p. 6 Paul J. Richards/AFP/Getty Images; pp. 8–9 corepics/Shutterstock.com; p. 10 Stephen Coburn/Shutterstock.com; pp. 12–13 David McNew/Getty Images; pp. 14–15 Greg Epperson/Aurora/Getty Images; pp. 28–29 John Warburton-Lee/AWL Images/Getty Images; p. 35 © Michael Newman/PhotoEdit; p. 37 © Cindy Charles/PhotoEdit; pp. 46–47 Robyn Beck/AFP/Getty Images; p. 49 Bounce/UpperCut Images/Getty Images; pp. 51, 52 Courtesy of John F. Boburchuk, Jr.; pp. 60–61 Kansas City Star/McClatchy-Tribune/Getty Images; pp. 62–63 © Ambient Images, Inc./SuperStock; pp. 64–65 Timothy A. Clary/AFP/Getty Images; back cover © iStockphoto.com/blackred.

Designer: Matt Cauli; Editor: Andrea Sclarow Paskoff; Photo Researcher: Marty Levick